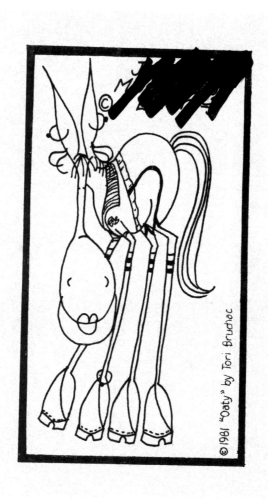

© 1981 "Oaty" by Tori Bruchac

First published 1982

Macdonald & Co
(Publishers) Ltd
Maxwell House
Worship Street
London EC2A 2EN

© Macdonald & Co
(Publishers) Ltd 1982

Adapted and published
in the United States by
Silver Burdett Company,
Morristown, N.J.

1983 Printing

ISBN 0-382-06694-4

Library of Congress
Catalog Card No. 83-60891

Editor
Lis Edwards

Production
Rosemary Bishop

Picture research
Caroline Mitchell

Illustrators
Angus McBride/Linden
Artists
Richard Hook/Temple Art
(*cover*)

The Art and Architecture Collection 19, 42(T)
Bibliothèque Nationale 8(T), 46(T)
The Bridgeman Art Library/Private Collection 47
British Museum 41
British Tourist Authority 48(TL)
J. Allan Cash Ltd 20
Mary Evans Picture Library 55
Fotomas Index 10
Giraudon 8(B), 29, 39, 53(T)
Koninklijk Museum, Antwerp 48(B)
Kunsthitstorisches Museum, Vienna 37

The Mansell Collection 54
MAS/Prado 30
The Master and Fellows of Magdalene College,
   Cambridge 12
Mauritshuis, The Hague 17
Metropolitan Museum of Art, New York 46(B)
Museum of London 36
National Maritime Museum 53(B)
The National Trust 48(TR)
Scala/Museum of San Martino, Naples 15
Stadelisches Kunstinstitut, Frankfurt 42(B)

Everyday Life
The Seventeenth Century

Laurence Taylor

Silver Burdett Company

The 17th century

In the 17th century Europe was divided as never before into two worlds – that of the rich and that of the poor. It was divided into a tiny world of privilege and wealth, and a huge world of poverty and suffering.

But the century was also one of strong religious faith. As in the 16th century Europe was still divided into two opposing religious camps. In the north the Protestant princes wanted to hold on to all the territories and peoples they had won during the Reformation. In the south, Roman Catholic countries, such as France, Spain and Austria led by the Pope, wanted to win back all the territory lost to the Church. After a long and bitter struggle both sides wearied of religious wars and a peace was signed. Yet Europe remained a battlefield for the 'super-powers' of France, Spain and Austria whose kings wanted to see their countries grow in power and glory.

It was a century of great artistic achievement. To the privileged world of Versailles, Louis XIV of France attracted all the great painters, sculptors and architects of the time. All over Europe beautiful houses were being built and richly decorated with the work of skilled artists and craftsmen.

While the arts flourished, so did science. The 17th century is famous for its 'Scientific Revolution'. For centuries men had believed that the earth was the centre of the universe. From this time onwards new discoveries about the universe we live in made it more and more difficult for men to accept this any longer. Great scientists like Galileo, Kepler and Newton had laid the basis for the modern world.

Contents

13808

The rulers

Louis XIV, King of France, was the most powerful ruler in Europe in the 17th century. To show off his power, he had a huge, splendid palace built at Versailles. The palace is richly decorated throughout with symbols of the King's power, like the sun. Louis even called himself *le Roi Soleil*, or 'the Sun King'.

Other European rulers tried to copy Louis. In England the Stuart King Charles II greatly admired him. But he knew that England was too poor to afford the great palaces, or large armies, which displayed the French King's power and wealth.

A great King in a splendid palace needed equally grand ceremonies to surround every moment of his life. Louis devised an elaborate ritual which was followed every day. From the moment he was woken up in the morning, to the time when he went to bed at night, his whole day was organised to impress on his subjects what it meant to be a King.

▲ The young Louis XIV dressed as the sun, for a Court masque. He was nicknamed the 'Sun King' (*Roi Soleil*).

▲ Louis XIV made his *levée* (getting up) into an elaborate ceremony. Nobles were specially chosen to attend him. Some only watched, but very favoured ones might be allowed to help Louis dress. The same thing happened when Louis went to bed.

◀ The splendid palace of Versailles was built for Louis XIV, to display his wealth and power. It is surrounded by enormous formal gardens, with fountains and lakes. Inside are many richly decorated rooms.

Many nobles disliked bowing and scraping. But they had to behave like this, or leave the Court. Louis was clever. He knew that if the great nobles were forced to spend all their money on clothes and entertainment, they would have none left to organise private armies. They would not be able to afford to plot against the King.

Towards the end of his reign France suffered greatly from Louis's ambitions. The Court at Versailles was very expensive. Louis's constant wars against other countries cost many thousands of lives and enormous sums of money. Even France could no longer afford the glory that Louis wanted.

The king's subjects

During the 17th century a new class was growing in society – the middle class. These people were below the King, nobles and gentry, yet clearly above the poor. They were either merchants or skilled craftsmen, or members of one of the professions – law, medicine, the army and the Church. The classes above and below them had a fixed social position, but the middle class could move. A few of its members climbed to the top, married into noble families, and became noble themselves. Most climbed up much more slowly, but they were still able to live comfortably.

At the very bottom there were many people struggling to become middle class. Some, by hard work and luck, managed to do so. Others failed, and remained poor.

Most people were poor. They had to pay heavy taxes to the King and to the Church, and to serve in the army. Although they produced much of the wealth in a country, they received few benefits.

► **Lesser nobles, gentlemen, army and navy officers**
Many of the lesser nobles and gentlemen were landlords, living in the country. The most senior officers in the army and navy (marshals and admirals) were usually great nobles.

◄ This is the title-page of a book written in 1600. It describes the life of an English gentleman.

► **King and queen**
Kings and queens were often very powerful. But many European rulers had to face serious rebellions. In England Charles I was beheaded (1649) after a successful rebellion by Parliament.

◀ *Thieves and beggars*

◀ *Labourers, cottagers and paupers*
Over half the population belonged to this group.

◀ *Farmers and freeholders*
These people paid most of the taxes.

◀ *Ordinary soldiers and seamen*
The lives of these men were harsh, and many more died of hunger and disease than in battle.

◀ *Artisans, craftsmen, shopkeepers and merchants*
Many were very poor; only a few became as rich as the nobles.

◀ *Clergy, doctors, lawyers, artists and scientists*
This group grew steadily as the demand for services increased.

▲ *Great nobles*
In every country rich and powerful men attended the king and queen. Some were given posts in the royal household. Some, including Archbishops and Bishops, acted as royal advisers.

The king's servants

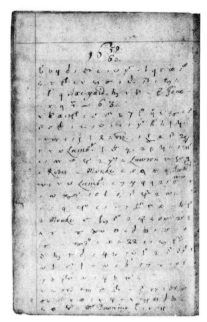

▲ The Englishman, Samuel Pepys, kept a fascinating diary of his life in 17th-century London. He wrote in a kind of shorthand, so you won't be able to read the page above.

▼ Part of London and the docks. Near the centre is the old St Paul's Cathedral.

At this time kings governed their countries. To help them make their countless decisions, they needed ministers who were properly trained, loyal and honest. Members of the king's own family, or of the older nobility, might use their power to intrigue and plot against him, so kings like Louis XIV chose middle-class men as their ministers. A king also needed a large number of administrators, or civil servants, to carry out his decisions.

In France powerful royal officers called 'intendants' were appointed to do this. But many other different kinds of servants were needed. Judges were appointed to punish and fine wrongdoers. Treasury officials arranged the collection of taxes, and ran a network of tax collectors which covered the country. Customs officers collected taxes on goods entering and leaving the country.

One loyal and hardworking civil servant was the Englishman, Samuel Pepys. He wrote a famous diary which, besides much else, tells us how he worked as the chief administrator of the Navy. As the civil servant in charge of the Navy, Pepys was responsible for organising and running the dockyards. These were where ships were built, refitted and prepared for war. Pepys carried out many reforms. He turned an inefficient and corrupt system of managing the dockyards into an efficient one. He also reformed the Navy, after it had been badly defeated by the Dutch in 1665.

For this work he has been called the Saviour of the Navy.

► Pepys lived in a fine house near the Navy Office in London. He often entertained his noble friends to excellent food and wine. After dinner his guests would sit down to play cards, or to look at his fine collection of pictures, books and furniture. Notice the model of a warship on the mantelpiece.

▼ Pepys had the important job of making sure that ships were ready to go to sea. He was in charge of buying stores of every sort, from sails, ropes, anchors and cables, to supplies of food and drink. He also had to order the press-ganging of sailors when ships were short of crews.

Religion, wars and rebellions

There were wars and rebellions almost every year in the 17th century. One of the longest and most destructive wars was the 'Thirty Years' War', from 1618 to 1648. It began as a struggle between the Protestants of Northern Europe and the Catholics of the South, but soon set Europe ablaze. By 1648 both sides were so war-weary and bankrupt that they made peace.

◄ People were not free to choose what religion they liked. This is an illegal meeting of Puritans, held in a barn, which is being broken up by soldiers.

▼ Soldiers were poorly disciplined, and badly paid and fed. They lived by plundering the country-side, ill-treating and killing those who tried to resist them, and burning their houses.

► This is part of a painting showing a revolt in Naples in 1647. It was led by a fisherman, Masaniello, and was in protest against high taxes.

Many of the civil wars and rebellions also began as struggles between Catholics and Protestants. The Protestant Dutch fought their Catholic Spanish masters for 80 years (1568 to 1648). They wanted to leave the Spanish Empire and become a free Protestant nation. The Catholic Irish bitterly resented their English Protestant overlords. In 1641 they rebelled violently against the injustices they suffered. In 1649, when the English Civil Wars were over, Oliver Cromwell went to Ireland to end their rebellion. Cromwell's troops massacred many townspeople. The memory of this has never been forgotten or forgiven.

In France, Louis XIV persecuted the Huguenots, who refused to give up their Protestant beliefs. Finally, in 1685, Louis forced over 200,000 Huguenots to leave France. Many of the refugees were skilled craftsmen, who were gladly received by other countries.

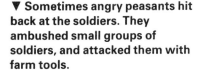

▼ Sometimes angry peasants hit back at the soldiers. They ambushed small groups of soldiers, and attacked them with farm tools.

Disease and medicine

Doctors' cures were often painful, and sometimes killed the patients. When King Charles II of England fell ill in 1685, twelve doctors treated him. First they took blood from his arm and made him violently sick. Then they shaved his head and applied 'blistering potions' to it. This was followed by 'gargles', more 'blood-letting', 'laxatives and draughts'. One remedy was made of 'forty drops of the spirit of human skull' in 'an ounce and a half of cordial jelup'. Obviously none of this was of any help to Charles and after four days he died.

Not all doctors were as ignorant as this. One of the most important discoveries in the history of medicine was made by the English doctor William Harvey. He proved that blood circulates through the body continuously, due to the pumping of the heart. But many doctors refused to accept such discoveries.

Plagues happened all over Europe during the 17th century. In 1603, 1625 and 1665 London was struck by the plague. The most severe outbreak was in 1665, when about 68,000 people died.

▲ Plague is caused by an invisible microbe, which attacks the black rat. Fleas live on the rat, and carry the disease to human beings by biting them. In the 17th century doctors and scientists did not know this.

Many towns and cities tried to stop the plague from spreading. In London, the sick were shut up in their homes for a month. Watchmen were placed outside to stop people from leaving or entering. The doors of all infected houses were marked with a large red cross. The dead had to be buried before sunrise or after sunset, in deep graves; householders had to keep the streets in front of their houses clean; stray dogs were killed, and no pigs or other animals were allowed within the city. The poor suffered most. Their houses were crowded and unhygienic, and disease spread quickly.

▼ The plague struck suddenly, and affected thousands. Whole families died, shut up in their homes.

▼ Red crosses were painted on the doors of houses where plague had struck warning passers-by.

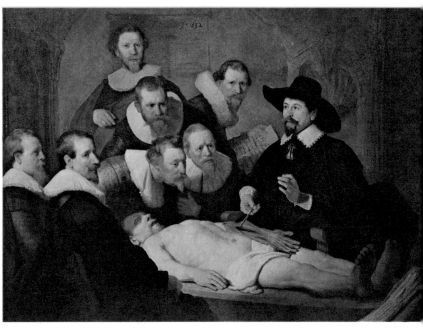

◄ Doctors tried to protect themselves against the disease. They wore long leather coats with hoods and gloves. The mask was stuffed with herbs, and the 'eyes' were made of glass.

▲Rembrandt painted *The Anatomy Lesson* in 1632. A doctor is dissecting a body in front of students. Everyone wears ordinary clothes, since nothing was known about germs.

▼ When plague broke out wealthy people fled from the city. Many left by boat to go to the country.

▼ The dead were buried either at night or early in the morning, when few people were about.

▼ The poor left on foot or by cart. They were often turned away from villagers fearing the plague.

▼ So many people died that great pits were dug to bury the bodies together.

The Great Fire of London

1665 and 1666 were unhappy years for the citizens of London. The plague of 1665 had hardly ended when a second disaster struck. This time it was a great fire. It started in a bakery in Pudding Lane, near London Bridge, on 2nd September 1666.

At first people living a little way off were not seriously worried. Samuel Pepys wrote in his *Diary* that his maid, Jane 'called us up about three in the morning, to tell us of a great fire in the City. So I rose . . . and went to her window . . . I thought it far enough off and so went to bed again to sleep'. But by the time Pepys awoke, later that morning, the fire had burnt down and completely destroyed over three hundred houses.

▼ As the fire spread through the narrow streets of the crowded city there was total panic. People struggled and fought to escape to safety across the river. The noise of the flames, the thick smoke and confusion was even more terrifying at night.

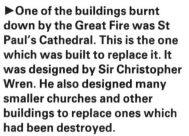

▶One of the buildings burnt down by the Great Fire was St Paul's Cathedral. This is the one which was built to replace it. It was designed by Sir Christopher Wren. He also designed many smaller churches and other buildings to replace ones which had been destroyed.

Later in the day Charles II ordered that houses in the path of the fire should be pulled down or blown up. But this did not stop it from spreading. By Monday, 3rd September, it had reached the centre of the City. Everywhere there were scenes of panic. The streets were jammed with people trying to escape, pushing handcarts and barrows, heaped high with their belongings. Even the Thames was packed with traffic, as boats ferried frightened people to safety on the south bank.

Four days later the fire had died down. It had destroyed over 13,000 houses and 87 churches, and had made thousands homeless.

But some good came of the Great Fire. It seems to have killed off the rats which carried the plague fleas, for the plague never visited London again.

Law and order

In 1630, in Milan, Italy, two men were accused of daubing someone's wall with cow-dung. They were tortured and confessed. They were ordered to be taken to the place of execution in a cart, their bodies struck with red-hot pokers as the cart moved through the streets, their hands chopped off, their bodies broken on the rack, their throats cut and their corpses burnt! Such horrific punishments were intended to terrify people watching as well as to punish the guilty. In many countries nearly every crime, particularly stealing, was punished by death. Men, women and children regularly went to watch these executions.

In the past, crime had been easier to deal with because towns and villages were smaller. Where everyone knew everybody else, it was much easier to track down wrong-doers. However, as the towns and cities grew, so did the number of criminals. Streets were poorly lit, and with no proper police force it was difficult to keep any sort of order, It was felt that the only way to deter criminals was to show that all crime would be severely punished.

▲ The corpses of thieves and robbers were left hanging in public places. These are the gallows at Inkpen Common, Berkshire.

◄Crimes were dealt with at several levels. The most serious ones, such as treason or rebellion, went to the court of the King's Bench (left). The Quarter Sessions (below left) dealt with all serious crimes except ones with a death penalty. The local Justices of the Peace met four times a year to try those cases. They were advised by a trained Clerk of the Peace, who sat below them. Each district had a Justice of the Peace (below). He dealt with some crimes in his own house.

◄In lonely parts of the countryside even large groups of travellers were not safe. Waggon trains were often attacked by gangs of disbanded soldiers.

▼The narrow, badly-lit streets of towns were especially dangerous at night. There were few watchmen, and muggings were common.

The changing landscape

As the population of Europe grew, so there were more and more people who needed food, clothing, fuel and shelter. To meet these needs more land had to be cleared on which crops could be grown and animals fed. Farmers also tried to produce more food on the same area of land.

Northern Europe had many woods and forests. Clearing the trees gave more land for farming. The trees provided wood for making things, and for fuel.

In many parts of Europe, farming land was made by draining low-lying, marshy areas. Drainage was expensive, but the land was very fertile.

Another way to improve the land was by 'enclosure'. This meant dividing land into smaller fields, by ditches and hedges. In most villages three kinds of land could be enclosed: the scrubby waste land outside the village, where the villagers collected wood for fuel; the common land, where they grazed their cows, sheep and geese; or the villagers' strips of land in the great open fields.

Only wealthy landowners could afford enclosure. Sometimes they paid the village farmers for the land they were taking away. At other times the landowners used force, and there were fierce battles as the villagers fought to protect their rights.

▲ Three stages in making charcoal. Charcoal, made from wood, was essential for making iron.
1. A round area was cleared and a pole put up in the centre.
2. The wood was arranged in a round stack, 3 metres high.
3. Turf was put on the outside. The stack burned slowly for 5 or 6 days.

► In many parts of the country landlords and village farmers stuck to the old farming methods. Corn and other crops were grown on narrow strips in open fields. Animals were grazed on the village meadows and surrounding commonland.

▲Reclaimed farmland in the Netherlands. This was a low-lying area in the north of Europe. The land was often flooded by the sea, so the Dutch became skilled at draining and building dykes to keep the sea back. Windmills helped to pump the water away.

◄Where the demand for corn, butter, milk and meat was growing, customs began to change. In this village the landlord and farmers have agreed to enclose the land. This will make larger fields, and improve the crops. What other changes can you see?

23

The farming year

▶ *Winter*
At this time of year the weather prevents work in the fields. But there is still plenty to do.

▶ *Autumn*
In southern Europe this is the time of the wine harvest, when the ripe grapes are picked and trampled to make wine. In other parts of Europe apples, pears and other fruits are picked and stored.

◄ Spring
This is a season of great
activity. Animals are put out to
fresh pasture, and shepherds are
busy lambing. Fields are
ploughed and sown. Children
scare birds away from the seeds.

◄ Summer
Everybody helps with the
harvest. The men cut the corn,
the women and children tie it into
sheaves and take it from the field
when it is dry. A good harvest
calls for great celebrations.

Gentlemen

Most of the countryside belonged to three kinds of people: kings, nobles, and gentlemen.

In almost every parish there was at least one gentleman, descended from a noble and ancient family. During the late 16th and early 17th centuries many gentlemen rebuilt their old semi-fortified houses. They added rooms, larger windows and more comfortable furniture. Gardens and lawns stretched in front of each house. Beyond them was parkland in which cattle and sheep grazed.

Close by the house was a sunny, walled kitchen garden. Nearby was the home farm. This provided meat, eggs, milk, cheese and butter for the gentleman's household.

The word 'gentleman' means that the person was 'gentle' born. Unlike people below them in social rank, gentlemen and their families did not have to work with their hands. Instead they could pay servants to work for them.

Together, the gentlemen and the nobles formed a rich and powerful group in the countryside. Most of the people below them worked for them and depended on them in one way or another.

►All over Europe nobles and gentlemen were building new, grander and more luxurious houses on their country estates. This is the first Eaton Hall in Cheshire, which was built at the end of the 17th century.

▼Three European gentlemen in typical 17th-century dress
1. An English gentleman 2. A French seigneur 3. A Spanish hidalgo.

1   2   3

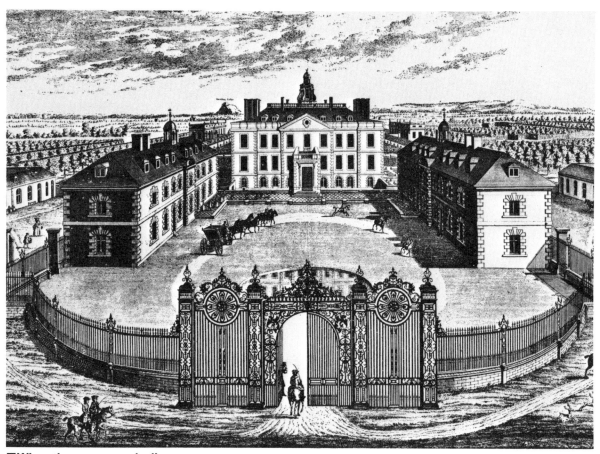

▼When they were not dealing
with estate business, or
upholding law and order,
gentlemen enjoyed hunting,
fishing and shooting. Here they
are shooting wildfowl.

A peasant's life

A peasant's life was short and hard. Both men and women had to work every day, all day, and most people died before they were 40.

Peasants did not own land. Sometimes, as in England, they paid rent to the landowner for farming part of his land. In France, some of the peasants were *metayers*. This meant that the landowner gave them land, seed, animals and tools. In return, at harvest time, they had to give the landowner half, or more, of what they had grown during the year. The poorest peasants were the day labourers. They had to find work every day, and were paid very little.

The main cause of the peasants' suffering was high taxation. There were many different taxes: taxes paid to the Church, taxes paid to the local lord, and, in France, a tax for using salt! Everything on the lord's land belonged to him. Peasants were not allowed to hunt game and could be sentenced to death if they were caught.

Some peasants did not farm, but had a trade. Most villages had a blacksmith and a wheelwright. In parts of the country where cloth was made, many people added to their income by working as spinners or weavers. They had more money than many peasant farmers. They had enough to eat, some furniture, a proper cottage, and some good clothes to wear on feastdays. But the poorer peasants lived miserably, especially in times of famine or war.

▶Poor peasant farmers, and their even poorer labourers, got up at dawn *(1)*. They worked all day in the fields *(2)* and came wearily home at sunset *(3)*.

Their homes were tumbledown and damp *(4)*. They had very little furniture. Poor farmers had to give much of what they grew as rent to the local lord *(5)*. Besides this they had to pay a tenth (tithe) of their produce of corn, wine, eggs and cheese to the local church *(6)*.

In the evenings poor families gathered round the fire for warmth *(7)*. They ate soup and bread most of the time.

▼Woollen cloth was England's biggest export in the 17th century. Most weavers worked in their own cottages. Women were not allowed to be weavers, because the looms were said to be too heavy for them to handle.

The woollen thread was brought to the weavers by middlemen, who came back to collect the cloth. These middlemen worked for wealthy merchants.

1

2

3

4

5

6

7

▼This painting by Michelin shows a baker's family in a small town in France. In the country people usually baked their own bread, but in towns they often bought it from a baker. They could also take food, such as meat, to be cooked for them in the baker's oven.

Growing up

Nearly half the people in Europe in the 17th century were less than sixteen years old. This was because people died much younger than they do now. Schools were expensive, so poor children often roamed in the streets all day. Tradesmen and wealthy farmers were able to afford to send their sons to school, and the very rich paid tutors to teach their children at home. Schools were rough, and children were severely punished for giving wrong answers or misbehaving. The main subjects were Latin, Greek and Religious Instruction.

Few girls went to school. They were trained to become housewives. Older girls had to look after younger children, and to help with all the household tasks, such as cooking, cleaning, mending and spinning. Boys helped their fathers, and so learned jobs such as ploughing, baking, weaving, shoeing horses or milling corn.

Because they started to work at an early age, children were treated more like grown-ups. Life was hard. Poor children had to work extremely long hours and were often sent away to work for wealthier families when they were eleven or twelve. Girls were trained as servants in the house, and boys as outdoor servants, such as stable-boys. Wealthy children studied much of the day.

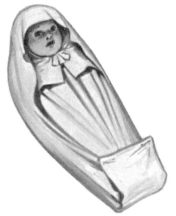

▲Babies were tightly wrapped in swaddling clothes. They slept in cradles like the one below.

▼A walking frame on wheels, very like ones used today.

◄Margarita Teresa, daughter of Philip IV of Spain, in 1656. She is wearing heavy clothes, like those of the adults.

Rocking horse

Toy gun

Doll

◄Some 17th-century toys.

►A young boy, wearing a dress. Boys and girls wore the same clothes till they were about six. Then boys were breeched (put into breeches). The father's clothes were fashionable in 1640.

▼Children learned their letters from a horn book like this. The letters are protected with a piece of transparent horn.

▼Many charity schools for poor boys and girls were founded at the end of the 17th century.

ABCDEFG
HIJKLMN
OPQRST
VUWXYZ
abcdefghij
klmnopqrſs
tvuwxyz&
A·E·I·O·U·Y

Costume and fashion

Poor children wore plain, hard-wearing clothes, very like those worn by their parents and grandparents. They did not own many clothes, and these had to last for a long time. Finer clothes were handed down from one generation to another. They were only worn on holidays. A man might own one hat, a doublet, a pair of leather breeches, a pair of woollen breeches, a jerkin, two shirts and two pairs of shoes. The very poor might just wear a long woollen or linen shirt, with leather sandals.

Rich people had far more clothes, and their styles often changed. Expensive jewellery and fashionable clothes showed how rich people were, but even fashionable people smelled strongly. Soap was expensive.

Traders brought new materials from abroad, such as muslin and cotton. Styles changed faster and faster, and sometimes became ridiculous. By the end of the century men looked as if they were in fancy dress, with wide, floppy hats, high-heeled boots, enormous wigs, and breeches covered with ribbons. Women made their waists tiny by wearing tight corsets, and decorated their faces with black patches, cut into fancy shapes.

▼Fashionable ladies wore elaborate make-up, and took a long time to dress. Their hair was curled, and parted in the middle. This style was brought to England by Charles I's French wife, Henrietta Maria. Faces were powdered, and cheeks rouged. Some ladies shaved off their eyebrows, and stuck on false ones made of mouse-skin! At one time there was a fashion for patches – fancy shapes cut out of black paper and stuck on to the face.

▼A beggar, dressed in rags and with bare feet.

▲Fashion in 1640. The man wears a high-fitting doublet, knee breeches, ruffled shirt-sleeves and a wide brimmed hat and plume. The lady's dress is high-waisted, with a low-necked bodice, trailing gown and full sleeves.

▼You can see a variety of fashions in this street, at the end of the century. The man is most fashionable, with his huge hat, large wig and lace cravat. He is also wearing petticoat breeches.

▲Puritans were strict Protestants, who believed that people should live simply. They disapproved of fashion, and wore plain, dark clothes.

Food and drink

For many people, food became more varied in the 17th century. The poor still lived mainly on bread and beer, but they ate meat and cheese more often. The meat was usually bacon. In the south of Europe they drank wine, rather than beer.

Richer people ate enormous amounts of meat. Vegetables were not very popular, and so constipation was common. Table manners were improving, and people used forks and spoons as well as knives. Poor people still ate off pewter or wooden plates, on a bare table. The rich now used china and glass, and covered their tables with linen cloths.

The explorers had brought new foods back from abroad. Potatoes came from South America. They became common at the end of the 17th century. They were a useful alternative to bread when grain was expensive.

The explorers also brought new drinks to Europe. At first only rich people could afford tea, coffee and chocolate (made from cacao). But as more of these were grown, so prices fell. By the end of the century tea- and coffee-drinking were common. Coffee-houses were opened in many towns and cities. Men went there to drink coffee, read news-sheets, discuss politics, do business and smoke their pipes.

▲A 'blackjack' (beer-jug) and mug. They are made of leather. The leather was softened in water, then shaped round a wooden block and sewn. It was set hard by boiling.

▶The dinner which Samuel Pepys served one day included two neats' tongues (ox tongues) and tanzy (a kind of pudding).

▲Wealthier families ate sitting at a simple table, made of long wooden boards. At meal-times this was covered with a white cloth. There was a lot of food, but few plates and dishes. Several courses were eaten off the same plate. Many people used only spoons and knives, but forks were becoming more common.

Carp

Salmon

Chickens

Tanzy

Neats' tongues

Cheese

◄The first coffee-houses were in Constantinople and Venice. In the mid-17th century coffee was brought to England. Soon there were coffee-houses in every town. The government tried to close them, because political meetings were held there.

►The 17th-century traders brought back many new goods from their voyages. It's hard to imagine life without potatoes, tea or coffee, but until this time Europeans had never tasted these everyday foods.

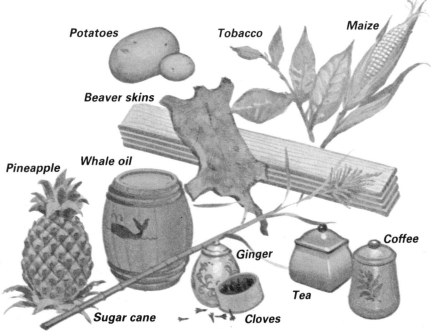

Potatoes

Tobacco

Maize

Beaver skins

Whale oil

Pineapple

Ginger

Coffee

Tea

Sugar cane

Cloves

Holy days and holidays

The great holiday of the year was called Carnival. This was the season from December to Lent, the time of fasting before Easter.

Carnival was a time when 'the World was turned upside down'. The poor were allowed to make fun of their betters without being punished. Everyone ate and drank enormously, and paraded through the streets in strange or ridiculous costumes.

There were other important festivals. On the first of May, to celebrate the coming of Spring and new life, there were noisy games, and people danced around the maypole. Another great festival was at harvest time, when feasting and dancing were followed by services of thanksgiving in churches.

Sports were part of holidays. Crowds flocked to see bears, bulls and boars being 'baited', snapped at by dogs. Cockfights were very popular. Running, jumping and wrestling contests were less cruel, but could be very noisy.

In England, Sunday afternoon was an opportunity for apprentices and workmen to play football. The ball was a blown-up pig's bladder. There were many players on each side, and people were often hurt. The game easily turned into a fight, and order had to be restored by the parish constable, or town watchman.

▼When the Thames froze over during the winter of 1683–84, a frost fair was held on the ice. Visitors from the country found it an extraordinary sight. The ice was so thick that fires could be burnt on it!

►Happy peasants dancing at a village fair, painted by the Flemish artist Bruegel. Fairs were held on feastdays and holy days, such as Easter. They gave people a chance to relax and enjoy themselves.

◄Cockfighting was a cruel sport. Sharp spurs were tied on to the birds' legs, and they fought to the death. The spectators laid bets on the birds. The ones which lost might be roasted alive by their disappointed owners.

▼Morris dances took place on feastdays, such as weddings and holy days. The dancers are brightly dressed, wear bells on their legs and wave handkerchiefs. One is wearing a hobbyhorse costume.

Entertainment for the rich

A favourite pastime of kings and their courts was hunting stags, wild boar and wolves. Hunting parties often stayed out all day. In the evening there was entertainment at the court; a ball or a party, a concert or a masque, and above all, gambling. Gambling was particularly popular at Versailles, which was nicknamed 'the gambling den'. Louis XIV himself disliked playing cards for long, and much preferred billiards.

The theatre was very fashionable, so nobles paid large sums of money to have their own boxes. They ate supper in their boxes, and played cards both before and after the performances.

Beneath the constant pleasure-seeking there was another, more desperate, side to the life of the nobles. They had to seek the king's favour all the time, so there was fierce rivalry among them. This often led to pointless quarrels, which were settled by duels, usually with swords. Duels frequently ended in serious wounds or even occasionally in loss of life.

▲ Pellmell was a game in which the players tried to hit a wooden ball through a hanging iron ring.

▼ A stag hunt arranged for the ladies of the Spanish Court. The animals are driven into a trap, and then killed.

◄Masques, balls and dancing were very popular with the nobles at court. In this painting you can see the musicians at the top on the left. The two dancers in front are about to lead a dance.

▼Some pastimes of the wealthy. Many gentlemen *(1)* enjoyed fishing.

Billiards *(2)* looked rather different, particularly with its curved cues.

Most people could play an instrument, or sing *(3)*.

Duelling *(4)* was discouraged. But it was still a common way to settle an argument.

1

2

3

4

The growing cities

Cities like London, Lisbon, Seville and Amsterdam were growing fast because they were on the main sea trade routes. Amsterdam was the wealthiest trading city. During the early 17th century more canals were dug, to allow ships to sail right into the city. The land between the canals was sold to merchants who built houses and warehouses along the canals. The city became known as the 'Venice of the North'.

Other cities, like Madrid, Vienna and Rome, grew because they were the centres of great empires. Rome contained the Vatican, which was the heart of the Roman Catholic Church. An enormous new church, St Peter's, was built there. It was meant to be a visible sign of the power of the Pope, Head of the Roman Catholic Church.

London was one of the busiest and most crowded cities of Europe. The Great Fire of 1666 destroyed many old buildings, and meant that much of the city could be re-designed. But King Charles II could not afford to rebuild on a grand scale. One of the most beautiful new buildings was St Paul's Cathedral. Parts of the rest of the city were rebuilt. Streets were widened, and new buildings could not be above a certain height. But London soon began to sprawl in all directions.

▼Amsterdam was a port, and its canal system was enlarged in the 17th century. This allowed ships to sail into the the city.

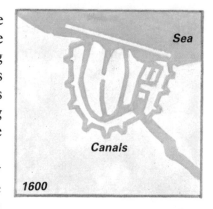

1600

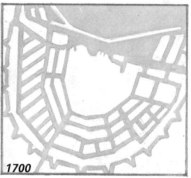

1700

▼This is the old London Bridge, which was burnt down in the Great Fire of London.

▲ In 1655 Gianlorenzo Bernini was commissioned by Pope Alexander VII to build a piazza in front of St Peter's. His vast square is one of the most exciting and dramatic sights in Europe.

Merchants and bankers

▼This splendid château was built for Nicholas Fouquet. It probably gave Louis XIV his first idea of what Versailles might look like.

Until the 17th century the nobles were the most important people after the king. Now groups of rich, powerful merchants were beginning to challenge the nobles. The merchants were important because they owned the ships which brought goods from all over the world to Europe. Inside Europe merchants controlled buying, selling and transport, and owned the workshops where goods were made.

Successful merchants became rich. Some merchants stopped trading and concentrated on lending money. They became bankers. Kings and nobles had to borrow money from them, so the bankers became very powerful. Some were employed by rulers to help collect taxes, and to manage the royal finances. One banker, Nicholas Fouquet, was Superintendent of Finances for Louis XIV. He became so rich that he could afford to build a magnificent chateau at Vaux-le-Vicomte. In 1661 Louis XIV was invited to a house-warming there. He was so jealous of Fouquet's grand house that he had him arrested!

▼By the 17th century the great merchants of Europe were trading to all parts of the known world. They became bankers as well as traders, lending and borrowing money. The coat of arms (*above*) was used by the East India Company, wealthy English traders.

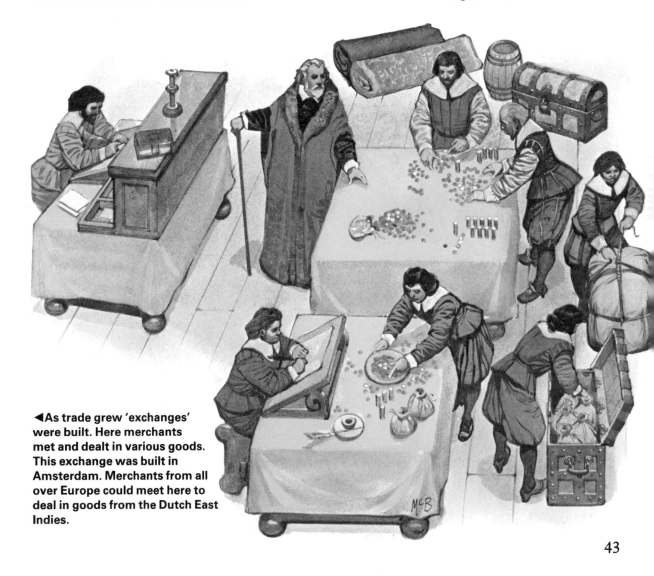

◄As trade grew 'exchanges' were built. Here merchants met and dealt in various goods. This exchange was built in Amsterdam. Merchants from all over Europe could meet here to deal in goods from the Dutch East Indies.

Craftsmen and workers

▼ Most goods were made and repaired by hand, by craftsmen. You would find all these people in any town.

▲ Making clothes was a slow job. The poor could not afford to buy fashionable and expensive clothes.

▲ Saddlers made and repaired harnesses and saddles. Horses were used for most forms of transport.

▲ You could not buy shoes ready-made. The shoemaker measured your foot, then made a pair of shoes to fit you.

▲ Wheelwrights made wheels for carts and coaches. Here one man is using a spokeshave to shape a spoke. Another is using a hand-drill, to make a hole to fit the axle.

▲ The knife-grinder (*right*) sharpened knives. He called at houses, and worked in the street.

▶ Goldsmiths usually worked together, in workshops like this. Apprentices worked for several years before they became skilled craftsmen.

There were no factories in the 17th century. Everything was made by hand, by thousands of craftsmen and less skilled workers.

Many of them were carpenters of some sort. Wood was used to make the framework of houses, and often the whole building. It was used to make ships and coaches, wheels and furniture, and even for the machinery in windmills and watermills.

Cloth-making was also a huge industry, throughout Europe. Weaving and spinning were done by thousands of workers in their own houses. The raw material was usually wool, flax or silk, but cotton was beginning to be imported from overseas. Spinning was done by women and children, but weaving was nearly always done by men. Once it had been woven the material was sent to highly skilled workers who dyed and finished it.

Most skilled craftsmen, making luxury goods, lived in towns and cities. They worked in workshops, like the famous glassworks of Venice, or the goldsmiths and silver-smiths in Florence. They made beautiful objects for rich people. The master craftsmen who owned these workshops employed a small number of workmen to help them. They usually had to serve a seven-year apprenticeship to learn their trade.

▲Town criers shouted out local news, and told people when events were happening.

▲People entertained themselves by singing popular songs. Song sheets were sold by street-sellers.

▲The ratcatcher carried a sign like this, to tell people what he did.

▲Porters carried goods, because many streets were too narrow for carts.

▲Small boys were employed by chimney sweeps to climb and clean chimneys.

The poor

Distribution du Pain du Roy au Louure

▲ There was a serious famine in France in 1693. The rich queued for bread, but the poor starved.

Poverty was a great problem in the 17th century. The population was growing very fast, and there was not enough work for everyone. Poor people wandered the countryside and towns, living by begging and stealing. Some of them were too ill or weak to work, and had no-one to look after them. Others were fit, but could not find work.

Beggars were cruelly treated. In England they were often whipped out of the parish and sent back to where they had come from. Some parishes put the poor into workhouses, which were more like prisons. This happened in France as well.

From time to time, when trade was bad, thousands of workers in the cloth industry lost their jobs. This meant that there were suddenly far more poor people moving around Europe, hungry and desperate. Famines made the problem worse, and there were often riots. The authorities were alarmed by public disorder, which could easily spread. In some places they gave food and clothes to the poor. In others, they treated the poor even more cruelly than before in an effort to get rid of them.

Sometimes wealthy people tried to help. They built almshouses, or they gave food and clothes to the poor on their land. But most poor people were not helped, and the problem of poverty remained.

◄ When harvests failed the price of bread rose. Poor people came to town to beg. Bread was a major part of their diet.

▼Many people wandered the country, like these Italian gypsies. They carried with them all that they owned.

▲Wealthy people often left money in their wills to build almshouses, in which old men and women could live free.

▼This is part of a painting called *The Tichborne Dole*. It shows a wealthy family giving food to the poor people of Tichborne.

Homes and gardens

A new style of building became popular during the 17th century. English architects, such as Inigo Jones who had studied abroad, were deeply impressed by the work of the great Italian architects of the Renaissance. Instead of building houses like the Elizabethan 'E'-shaped mansions, everything was made to run in a straight line along the front of the building. Houses became more box-like, with sloping roofs and plain rectangular windows. Inside, the rooms were small and regular.

The rich planned formal gardens round their new houses. Flower gardens were arranged in rectangles and squares, divided by broad walks, and often had a sundial in the centre. Box or lavender hedges were trimmed into ornamental shapes, or planted as mazes.

Gardening was made popular in England by Protestants who had fled from the religious wars in the Netherlands in the 1560s. They brought with them many new plants, such as tulips, laburnum, nasturtiums and love-in-the-mist.

By the end of the century more natural gardens were being designed. This was the beginning of landscape gardening.

▲ Three kinds of 17th-century chairs.

▼The plan of yeoman William Wilkes's house, taken from an inventory made after his death in 1608. The inventory listed what he owned, and how much everything was worth.

1. Hall
2. Parlour
3. Room over parlour
4. Kitchen
5. Buttery entry
6. Dairy
7. Room over hall
8. Buttery
9. Maid's room
10. Room over entry
11. Cheese room
12. Granary

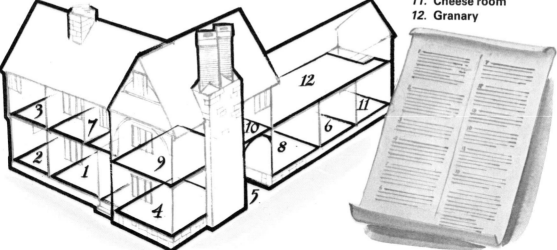

▲The Englishman Grinling Gibbons was a wonderfully skilled woodcarver. His delicate wood carvings of fruit and flowers look very realistic. They particularly delighted Charles II, who became one of his patrons.

▼At the beginning of the 17th century gardens were still very formal. This French painting shows the activities in a large garden in spring. You can see that the flowerbeds are arranged in a geometric pattern, divided by low hedges.

▲The Queen's House at Greenwich was designed by Inigo Jones and built between 1616 and 1635. Its clear-cut outline and beautiful proportions brought the style of the Italian Renaissance to England.

Travel and communication

Most people did not travel far from their homes unless they had to. Travel was slow, uncomfortable and often dangerous. In bad weather rivers could sweep away bridges, halt ferries and turn roads into swamps. Snowstorms and snowdrifts could block roads for days, even weeks. Footpads, highwaymen and bandits lay in wait as a constant threat to travellers.

The most common form of transport was on horseback. Poor people walked, or travelled in goods waggons. These were huge and heavy. Each was drawn by a team of twelve horses, and could only go at about three miles (5 km) an hour, or walking speed. Stage-coaches were gradually coming into use, but they were expensive and uncomfortable. Only the rich could afford to use them. The fastest means of transport was the letter-post. But even this varied with the weather. The postal service across Europe, from Lisbon to Danzig on the Baltic coast, could take somewhere between thirteen and 53 days to cover the 2000 miles (3200 kilometres).

By the end of the century lighter and faster passenger-carrying vehicles began to appear.

▲In the 1640s it took ten days to send letters privately from London to Edinburgh by mounted post boy. The cost depended on the number of pages sent.

▼Travellers had to pay a toll when they crossed someone's land. The tolls were collected at tollgates, like this one. The tollgate-keeper lived in the house next to the tollgate.

50

◄This is a litter. It was either carried by men or had a horse at the front and back. It had a light wooden framework covered with leather.

▲Only rich families could afford to keep a coach, horses and driver. The windows had no glass, and there were few springs.

▲Many goods were carried on open carts like this one. They were pulled by strong farmhorses and led by a carter.

▲Some pack-horses, laden with goods, are crossing a bridge. One barge is carrying coals. The 'tilt boat', with a canopy, carries passengers.

▼This is a stage waggon, for passengers. It was an ordinary cart, covered with cloth to keep the rain out. A heavy load could need up to six horses.

Machines and inventions

◄ Guns became safer, faster and more accurate in the 17th century. This is a flintlock pistol. The flintlock firing mechanism was safer than the matchlock (*above*) and gradually replaced it.

In the 17th century, people thought hard about how to make machines more powerful and efficient.

One source of energy was the wind. A new type of mill was designed. This was the tower-mill, which gave more power than the old post-mill. Unlike the post-mill, only the top of the tower-mill, to which the sails were attached, moved. As the machinery did not move with the sails, much larger, more powerful mills could be built. They were used not just for grinding corn but also for pumping water, crushing seed for oil, making gunpowder and pulping rags into paper.

Water-power was also improved. Water-wheels were used for splitting iron rods, working tilt hammers in forges and powering the machinery in silk mills.

Industries such as clockmaking and printing were speeded up so that more goods could be produced. In the past, a few skilled craftsmen had made a clock or book. Now the process was broken up into many different tasks. Each workman did one task, such as making the type, typesetting, printing or binding the book. It took less time to make each book, and more could be made.

Blast furnaces became much larger. This meant that more iron was used, particularly to make weapons of war. Guns were made more precisely and became more accurate. This was to change warfare completely.

▲ As the houses of the wealthy held more and more precious objects, they had to be protected. Ingenious and highly decorated locks were made, like this one.

►The waterworks at Marly-sur-Seine. This was the biggest water-wheel machine ever constructed. It was built for Louis XIV, to supply the fountains at the palace of Versailles.

▼A travelling clock, made with a special balance-wheel so that it would keep time when moving.

►The first Eddystone lighthouse, built at the end of the 17th century. It was destroyed in a great storm in 1703.

▼The 'Sovereign of the Seas' was built in 1637, in England. She was the first boat to carry royals and top-gallants on all masts. The Dutch called her the 'Golden Devil', because there was so much carving and gilding on her stern.

Scientific advances

▼ This detailed drawing of a flea comes from a book called *Micrographia* by the 17th-century scientist Robert Hooke. He made his own microscope (*below*) and drew what he saw through it. This was the first book written about using microscopes.

Hooke was one of the founding members of the Royal Society. This was a group of men who met to hear scientific lectures. Some other famous members were Sir Christopher Wren, Sir Isaac Newton, Samuel Pepys, the chemist Robert Boyle, and John Evelyn, another diarist.

During the 17th century people gradually realised that the old superstitious explanations of the world did not fit the facts that were being discovered about it. Scientists began to do careful experiments, observing and recording the results before coming to any conclusions. Many of their discoveries were different from the Church's view of the world. Because of this, many scientists were attacked by the Church. For example, the Italian astronomer Galileo said that the earth went round the sun, not the other way round. In 1633 he was placed under house arrest for the rest of his life, and prevented from publishing his ideas.

Although the Church silenced some scientists, it could not stop the advance of science throughout Europe. Astronomers like the German Johann Kepler, the Dane Tycho Brahe, and Hevelius of Danzig, as well as mathematicians like the Frenchmen Descartes and Pascal, all transformed scientific knowledge.

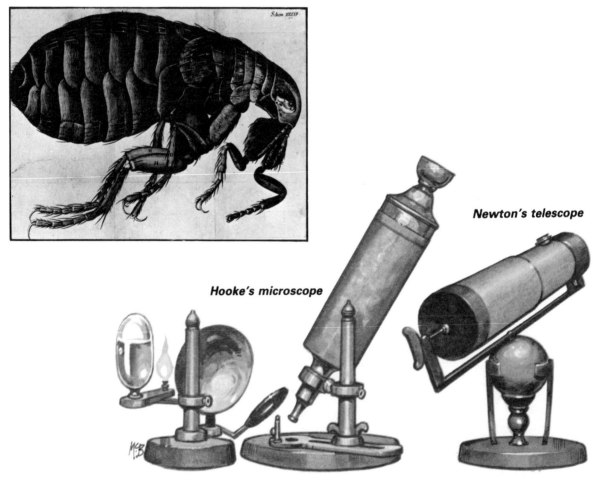

Newton's telescope

Hooke's microscope

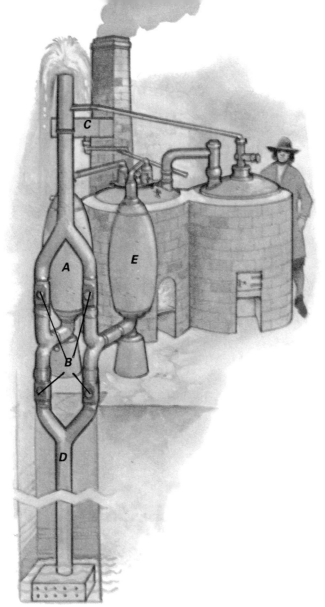

◀This is the first steam engine, designed by Thomas Savery in 1698. It was used for pumping water out of mines. This meant that mine shafts could be dug much deeper, without being flooded.

1. Steam enters the container A. Water is displaced up through valves B.
2. When all the water has left A, steam stops coming in. Cold water is poured on to A from the cistern C.
3. The cold water condenses the steam in A. This creates a vacuum, drawing water up through the pipe D, through the valves B.
The same process happens in the other container E, while A is cooling.

◀Astronomy became a science in the 17th century. Stronger, more accurate telescopes meant that astronomers could make exact observations. This is the Royal Observatory at Greenwich.

Europe overseas

▼Most European settlements in America were near the coast or in river valleys. This was because it was difficult and dangerous to travel overland. The foreign explorers and settlers claimed land which was not theirs, so they had to fight the natives all the time.

By the end of the 17th century Europe was linked to most of the known world by ties of settlement, trade and religion. In South and Central America the Spanish and Portuguese made enormous conquests. The Dutch had valuable trading stations in the East Indies. Britain and France struggled to establish settlements in North America and trading posts in India. Many young men went to these colonies to make their fortunes. Land there was cheap, and so were people to work on it.

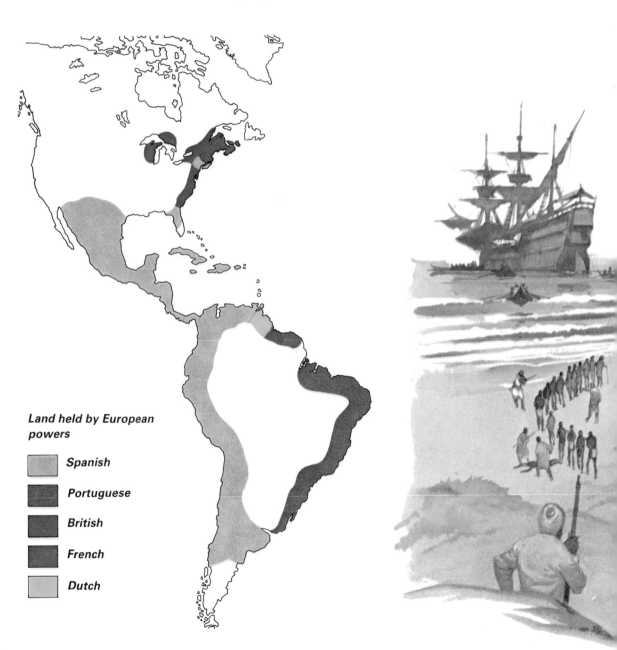

Land held by European powers

	Spanish
	Portuguese
	British
	French
	Dutch

▲A fort in New England being attacked by Indians. There were many wars between the settlers and the Indians, whose land they took.

▼Arab slave traders in West Africa selling slaves to an English captain, who will sell them to settlers in the New World. There the slaves will have to work for nothing on the plantations.

From this time onwards the European countries ruled over other peoples of many different races and religions. These peoples were often forced to adopt the language, customs and religious beliefs of their European rulers.

Many of these peoples were badly treated, because they were seen as inferior to Europeans. They had to work long hours in gold and silver mines, or on plantations. Many of them were slaves, brought from Africa, who had no rights at all.

57

Main events

1600 The English East India Company was founded.

1603 Elizabeth I of England died. James VI of Scotland, the son of Mary Queen of Scots, became King James I of England.

1605 Catholic plotters, led by Guy Fawkes, tried to blow up the Houses of Parliament. They failed.

1607 One hundred and four Englishmen established the first permanent English settlement in North America at Jamestown, Virginia.

1609 A twelve years' truce was signed between the Spaniards and their rebellious Dutch subjects.

1618 The beginning of the 30 Years' War which was to involve almost every country in Europe.

1620 The Pilgrim Fathers sailed across the Atlantic in the *Mayflower* and settled in Plymouth, Massachusetts.

1624 Richelieu, one of the most famous of all French ministers, entered King Louis XIII's Council.

1625 James I died and was succeeded by his eldest son Charles I. Both kings faced great hostility from Parliament.

1628 In France Huguenot (Protestant) rebels were defeated by Richelieu at La Rochelle.

1629 Charles I dissolved Parliament. For eleven years the King tried to rule the country without Parliament.

1630 English Puritans (extreme Protestants) who disagreed with Charles I, began a migration to North America. By 1643 some 65,000 had left the country.

1641 A savage civil war started in Ireland. The Catholics struggled to drive out their English Protestant landlords.

1641 The English Parliament which had been recalled by Charles ordered the execution of his chief minister the Earl of Strafford.

1642 The start of the English Civil Wars. Both Parliament and Charles I prepared for battle.

1643 Louis XIII of France died. Ann of Austria, his widow, became regent as Louis XIV, her son, was still a child.

1645 Battle of Naseby. The Royalist Army was finally defeated by the armies of Parliament.

1646 The end of the English Civil Wars. Charles I escaped to Scotland, but was later handed back to the Parliamentary Army.

1648 The Treaty of Westphalia ended the 30 Years' War in Europe. The same year Holland finally won its independence from Spain.
The Frondes in France. This was a revolt of the nobles and middle-class against the unpopular regent Ann of Austria and her Minister Mazarin.

1652 The Protestant English started a war against the Protestant Dutch. Bitter rivalries had grown up between the two countries over fishing rights, trade and colonies.

1653 Oliver Cromwell became Lord Protector of England.

1658 Cromwell died.

1660 In England the rule of Parliament ended. It had always been unpopular with the Royalists and also with many ordinary people. Charles II, the son of Charles I, returned to England amid great rejoicing.

1661 Louis XIV came of age and began his long reign.

1665 Plague spreads through London.

1666 The Great Fire of London.

1667 During the Second English War against the Dutch, a fleet under the Dutch Admiral De Reuter sailed up the Thames and the Medway and burnt a number of warships.

1670 Charles II signed a secret treaty with Louis XIV. In return for badly needed cash, Charles agreed to support Louis against the Dutch.

1672 The Third Dutch War. Under the Secret Treaty of Dover England was allied with France against its old rivals the Dutch.

1679 Because it disliked Catholics, Parliament passed a bill to exclude the King's brother James, a suspected Catholic, from the throne.

1683 Death of Colbert, for twenty years Louis XIV's great Minister of Finance.

1685 James, Duke of York, becomes King of England on the death of his brother Charles II.
Louis XIV disliked the Huguenots (French Protestants) and drove about 200,000 out of France.

1688 James II was forced to give up the throne of England. He had favoured Catholics in the Government, Army and Church. William of Orange and his wife Mary (daughter of James II) were invited to succeed James as William III and Mary II.

1694 Queen Mary II died.

1700 Death of King Charles II of Spain. Louis XIV claimed the throne of Spain for France, starting a great European war which lasted until 1714.

1702 Death of William III. He was succeeded by Queen Anne.

Ann of Austria was the mother of Louis XIV. After the death of her husband, Louis XIII, in 1643, Ann became Regent of France. She was helped by another great minister, Mazarin.

Anne was Queen of England and the last of the Stuart line. A very ordinary woman, Anne succeeded William III, the husband of her childless sister Mary. Britain's empire grew rapidly in her reign from 1702 until 1714.

Duke of Buckingham was the favourite of James I and then Charles I. He rose rapidly to fame and fortune after 1618. He was hated by the King's enemies in Parliament and was assassinated in 1628.

Charles I was unable to keep out of foreign quarrels or to solve his problems at home in England. By 1640 he was quarrelling bitterly with Parliament. Both sides went to war in 1642. Charles's army was defeated in 1645 and he was beheaded in 1649.

Charles II fled from England after the defeat of the Royalist army at Worcester in 1651. He returned to great celebrations in 1660 when it was clear there was nobody to follow Cromwell. All his reign Charles tried to avoid another Civil War. He died in 1685.

Colbert was Louis XIV's great financial minister. Colbert carried out many reforms. It was he who created the wealth that Louis XIV spent.

Cromwell was an enemy of Charles I. Oliver Cromwell first became leader of Parliament's New Model Army in the Civil

War and then became ruler of the country. He was the first uncrowned ruler of England.

Galileo Galilei built one of the first telescopes in 1609. He was a great Italian scientist, but because the Catholic Church thought his ideas about the universe were too dangerous and unsettling he was put on trial for heresy. To save his life he agreed that his ideas were misleading.

William Harvey was able to show how blood circulates through the body by examining the hearts of animals. His discovery marks the beginning of modern medicine. He died in 1657.

Henrietta Maria was the sister of Louis XIII, the wife of Charles I and mother of Charles II and James II. She was disliked in England as she was both a Roman Catholic and pro-French. She died in 1669.

James I was the son of Mary Queen of Scots, beheaded by her cousin Queen Elizabeth I in 1587. James was already King of Scotland when he succeeded to the English throne in 1603. He died in 1625.

James II was disliked because it was believed he was a secret Catholic. When he came to the throne after his brother Charles's death in 1685 he showed great favouritism to Catholics. He was allowed to flee the country in 1688.

Johann Kepler believed that the sun was at the centre of the universe and not the earth. However, after many years of patient work, Kepler showed that the planets did not orbit the sun, but travelled around it in elipses. He died in 1630.

Louis XIV was King of France and the most powerful ruler in Europe. The years of his reign are known as 'Le Grand Siècle' (The Great Century). Under him France led the western world in art, architecture and literature. Until constant wars ruined the country, it was also very rich in people and resources.

Mary II was cursed by her father James II after he had fled from England and she and her husband became King and Queen of England. She was very popular and helped William who was a cold man.

Sir Isaac Newton was one of England's greatest scientific geniuses. Newton discovered the laws of gravitation and of bodies in motion. This helped explain why the stars and planets stay in the sky. He died in 1727.

Rembrandt van Rijn was one of the greatest artists of all times. Rembrandt was Dutch, a brilliant drawer and a wonderful portrait painter.

Richelieu was one of the great ministers of France. From 1624 until his death Cardinal Richelieu served his master Louis XIII of France well. His greatest work was to destroy the power of the French nobles and to increase the King's power.

Sir Christopher Wren was the famous English architect who rebuilt St Paul's and many other City churches after the Fire of London. Wren's most glorious achievement was the great dome of St Paul's. He died in 1723.

William III was married to James II's Protestant daughter Mary. He was a great Dutch war-leader and a Protestant. He was, therefore, a very suitable person to become King of England. He agreed to work with Parliament and not against it. He spent most of his reign fighting wars against Louis XIV.

Glossary

carnival The season of festivities before the forty days of fasting ordered by the Church from Ash Wednesday to Easter.

dyke A wall built to keep the sea from flooding land or, a large ditch or canal dug to drain marshy land.

flax A plant with a long stem and blue flower. Its fibres are used for making linen.

Huguenot A French Protestant (*see* Protestant).

intendant An important servant of the king in France, Spain and Portugal, who was given great power.

linen A cloth made from threads spun from flax. A very common material before cotton was widely used.

masque A play or entertainment where the actors hid their faces with masks.

Protestant A member of one of the churches led by those reformers (such as Luther, Calvin, Zwingli) who disagreed with the practices of the Catholic Church. In England extreme Protestants were often called 'Puritans' because they wanted to 'purify' the English Church of all Roman Catholic practices and beliefs.

rack An instrument of torture on which a victim's body was stretched in order to make them confess a crime.

reform To improve or to change for the better things that are unsatisfactory, wrong or evil.

Renaissance A French word which means re-birth. It is used to describe the great interest people in the 15th and 16th centuries showed in the ancient Greeks and Romans.

Index